HAMS S

The Hamste e

Hamsters: The Hamster Care Guide by Louisa Tarver

Contents

WHAT ARE HAMSTERS?

Hamsters are small rodents that resemble mice, but they have rounder bodies and shorter tails.

The most common species of hamster is the Syrian or golden hamster, but there are multiple other species as well. They can live up to 3 years and can be anywhere from 2-10 inches long depending on their breed.

When it comes to hamsters as pets, there are many reasons why they make good companions. These cute creatures make great pet animals because they are small enough to keep in most living spaces, they sleep late in the day, and they are very friendly.

Hamsters are typically less than 6 inches long, making them easy to transport. In addition, hamsters like to exercise by running around on wheels or climbing through tunnels. This makes them great for people who want an active and entertaining pet.

Finally, hamsters are easy to care for because they don't require a complicated diet. Their requirements are plentiful but quite simple.

All these factors make hamsters perfect pets! Hamsters can be purchased from a local pet store. You should always purchase healthy hamsters that appear happy and well-fed.

Many people choose to adopt a hamster as their new pet, but how do you know if this is the right choice for you?

First, it's important to think about your living situation. A hamster is a great choice if you live in an apartment as they don't take up much space.

Next, consider whether or not you have enough time to provide adequate attention for your hamster.

Finally, make sure that you can handle any potential health problems that may arise from owning a hamster.

If all these factors are met, then by all means go ahead and adopt one!

Hamsters are very social animals who enjoy being with other people. They also love toys so be prepared to spend some money on them when you bring your little friend home.

WHY HAMSTERS MAKE GOOD PETS

When it comes to choosing the perfect pet, there are all sorts of options. Dogs, cats, fish, birds - the list goes on. But if you're looking for a pet that is low-maintenance and just plain cute, then hamsters might be the right fit for you! One might say that the best pet is one who provides companionship with their personality, and these furry little guys certainly do that! Though they are small in size, they are still able to provide companionship with their cute personalities. Here are some reasons why these furry little guys make great pets:

- Hamsters make great pets because they are low-maintenance and generally don't require as much attention as other animals, such as dogs or cats.
- Hamsters are also very clean creatures so you don't have to worry about them making a mess in your home! You can usually handle them without too much risk of being bitten.
- They are fairly quiet, so if you live in an apartment building where other tenants might complain about animal noises, this might be a good option for you.
- Hamsters are also very cute pets that will provide you with hours of entertainment just by watching them run around their cages or play with toys.
- They're small enough - typically six inches long - to easily hold in your hand, but large enough for you to feel like you're

doing something productive when taking care of them.

- They also come in many different colours and patterns!
- Hamsters make great beginner animals for kids because they require little attention and can easily be taken care of by a child.
- They don't need to be walked or fed special food.
- They live around two to three years which is pretty long for a small animal.
- You can also teach them to do tricks like rollover or play dead, which is always fun.
- Hamsters are also relatively inexpensive when it comes to buying and feeding them.
- Hamsters are generally friendly animals and happy if you give them attention.

Hamsters are nocturnal by nature so you might not get as much sleep while caring for them if they're placed too near bedrooms or you live in a small apartment. This is because they spend a lot of time exercising so making sure your hamster wheel doesn't squeak will help you to sleep better!

Hamsters make such popular pets because they are such easy animals to care for. They require a small environment and a small amount of food and water. They also don't need a lot of space and they're inexpensive to purchase.

If you want a pet that doesn't require a lot of work and responsibility, then a hamster might be the perfect pet for you!

CHEEK POUCHES

Hamsters have cheek pouches which are used in the wild to transport food back to their burrows. You may find they hide food amongst their bedding in the same way in their cage.

The pouches are strategically located on the sides of their face so that they can use their mouths to continue to chew food while carrying it back to the burrow. They spend a lot of time foraging for food during the night, storing it in these cheek pouches for later consumption.

For an animal that never seems to stop eating, it can be tough to figure out just how much food a hamster can store in its cheek pouches. One thing is for sure, however: they have a lot of storage capacity! A single cheek pouch can hold up to four tablespoons of food, which is comparable to the size of a walnut.

It's not hard to imagine that once they've filled them up, their cheeks are quite heavy. The more often a hamster feeds, the more food it will store. This can become a problem in captivity as a hamster may not need to eat as often as it does in its natural environment but will still hoard food in its cheeks each time it eats.

A hamster's cheeks can become so full that it cannot empty them properly leading to spoiled food and possible infection or illness.

TEETH

Hamsters teeth never stop growing and they have to chew constantly to keep their teeth from overgrowing.

The best type of hamster food for this is pellets or treat sticks made specifically for this purpose.

Pellet mixes are specially formulated to contain all of the nutrients a hamster needs, as well as being hard for the hamster to chew on.

Treat sticks are made from compressed nuts and seeds that your hamster will gnaw away at slowly, helping wear down their teeth in the process.

HIBERNATION

Hamsters are permissive hibernators meaning they will hibernate if environmental conditions require it. This is usually in cold temperatures but can also be if temperatures are too hot or if there is a food or water shortage.

Contrary to obligatory hibernators who fatten themselves up to survive colder winters, hamsters can hibernate whenever it is required throughout the year because of poor environmental conditions.

It is very unusual for a hamster kept in captivity indoors to hibernate if food supply and temperatures are stable.

The first signs of hibernation are usually regular periods of lethargy, less appetite, and decreased activity followed by more regular periods of lethargy, less appetite, and decreased activity until the animal is completely immobile.

If you believe your hamster is about to hibernate, it's important that you act fast to determine the cause. Your hamster will be happiest with a consistent temperature and adequate food and water supply. If any of these conditions are not being met you may experience your hamster hibernating.

Ensure the cage is not near a source of heat or cold such as a window or radiator and make sure that nothing is stopping your hamster from getting to their food or water.

If your hamster remains lethargic you should consult your veterinarian.

SLEEPING HABITS

Hamsters are nocturnal animals which means they prefer sleeping during daylight hours and are active at night.

They can be quite noisy at night as they go about their activities of eating, drinking water, grooming themselves, and playing with toys. The noise level varies depending on how many hamsters there are in one cage. It is not advisable to keep hamsters in a bedroom for this reason.

Hamster cages should be kept away from the main sleeping areas so that they do not disturb your family members while you sleep. You should place the cage where it will not bother anyone else when you're asleep.

Hamsters will usually wake up once the lights are turned off.

EXERCISE

Hamsters are primarily burrowing animals who spend most of their day underground. However, hamsters have been known to exhibit an instinct to climb when they feel threatened or anxious. This is particularly true for young hamsters, who may climb up to the top of their cage to escape an older or more vicious hamster; in this way, climbing can help to relieve the stress that the young animal might be feeling.

You may find your hamster has become an acrobat and is climbing the bars of its cage or perhaps dangling from the roof! This is quite common behaviour which is usually because they have so much energy. However, there are times when this behaviour is because the hamster is trying to get away from something lower in the cage that is causing them stress or because they are bored.

Make sure that their wheel can spin freely and is not trapped and that their cage does not need cleaning. If another hamster shares the cage make sure they are not fighting or causing each other stress.

EXERCISE WHEELS

Hamsters are very active animals and can travel miles in the wild during the night.

They have a lot of energy and so need a way to burn this off in their cages.

Hamsters love to run on wheels. When they start running, they run at a speed of 5 kilometres an hour (3.1 miles).

HAMSTER DIET

Hamsters need a balanced diet that includes proteins, vegetables, and fruits.

Many people don't realise that hamsters are omnivores which means they are meat-eaters. In the wild, this comes in the form of the occasional insect but they get much of their protein from nuts or seeds. They commonly eat grain, seeds, and fresh vegetables like carrots, celery, lettuce, spinach, kale, and cabbage.

The way you feed your hamster will have a major effect on his or her health. Hamsters that are not fed the right diet can develop health problems such as obesity, diabetes, and kidney failure.

It is important to always consider the size of your hamster when giving treats. What may seem like a small amount of salt, sugar, or fat content to us is a huge amount for a tiny hamster who'll happily eat their sugary snack, even if it's bad for them. The sugars in just a quarter of an apple for instance are a massive amount for a small hamster to consume in one day.

Pellets Vs. Seed Mix

Hamster pellets vs. seed mix is a debate that has been going on for a while. Some people say that feeding your hamster a pellet-based diet is the only way to go because it's scientifically formulated and better for them, while others think seed-mixes are healthier and offer more variety in flavour and nutrients.

Contrary to popular belief, dry hamster pellets are quite good for your hamster! Hamsters love the taste of these pellets and they are very nutritious for them. It's important to have some on hand so you can feed your pet any time it needs a little extra food.

Introducing New Foods

The best way to introduce new foods into your hamster's diet is to only give something new every few days. This allows plenty of time to pick up on any ill effects and notice any intolerances your hamster may have to the food given.

Fresh Food

When giving fresh food it is important not to give too much at once due to a hamster's natural instinct to hoard. The food could spoil in their cheeks or they may hide it amongst their bedding where it can go bad. Regular cage cleaning is especially important if you are giving your hamster fresh food.

Fruit

Fruits contain nutrients and fibre that help your hamsters digestion. Due to its high sugar content fruit should be an

occasional treat for your hamster and only a small amount should be given a couple of times a week. Fruits that are lower in sugar are best such as apples, pears, strawberries, peaches, and kiwis.

Citrus fruits shouldn't be given to your hamster as they can lead to tummy upsets and also have high sugar contents.

Vegetables

Many vegetables can be included in your hamster's diet. Some popular ones are:

- Carrots - carrots provide the essential nutrients needed for a healthy hamster. They also help with dental health as all the chewing keeps teeth clean and stops them from getting too long.
- Broccoli
- Spinach
- Cauliflower
- Zucchini

Protein

Dry hamster pellets are formulated to include protein so if you are feeding this to your hamster you don't need to add any extra protein to their diet. If you want to feed your hamster proteins then the following are some safe and popular choices:

Plant-based proteins include:

- Beans
- Lentils
- Peanut butter - avoid any with added sugar and give as an occasional treat due to its high fat and salt content.
- Chickpeas
- Tofu
- Seeds, nuts and grains

Animal-based proteins:

- Eggs - boiled or scrambled
- Cheese - hard or soft
- Dried Mealworms - these can be purchased from pet shops.

Cheese & Dairy

Most hamsters are fine eating a small amount of cheese or dairy as an occasional treat & many love the taste. However, it is not uncommon for a hamster to have a dairy intolerance, so you should keep a close eye on your hamster after giving them cheese or dairy the first few times. Some hamsters may suffer from loose stools & you should keep an eye on their food bowl to make sure they are still eating & not suffering from a stomach ache. Cheese is high in fat and salt content so you should limit cheese to a pea-sized amount a couple of times a week.

TYPES OF HAMSTER & THEIR CHARACTERISTICS

Hamsters are beloved by pet owners for their curiosity, cuteness and the ease with which they can be kept as pets.

With more than 20 types of hamsters, it can be difficult to decide on the type of animal that's right for you! Here we will explore some of the most popular kinds to keep as pets, along with their distinctive traits. We hope this information helps you make an informed decision about your new furry friend.

Keeping More Than One Hamster

If you intend to have multiple hamsters in one cage, make sure that you know their gender and keep males and females apart.

Golden hamsters should always be kept on their own but most dwarf hamsters are happy to live together, especially if raised together from birth.

You should not mix different breeds of hamster in the same cage. They may fight and often have different dietary needs and preferences.

GOLDEN HAMSTERS

Golden hamsters are also known as Syrian hamsters and are the most common hamsters kept as pets. They are best kept alone and may fight or become stressed if kept together.

Long haired golden hamsters are known as teddy bear hamsters because of their cute and fluffy appearance.

Golden hamsters have decreased in number in the wild over the past few decades due to the decline of their natural habitat. They are now considered to be vulnerable in the wild.

They are very playful animals that can weigh up to 150 grams and grow to around 6 inches in length.

They have a great ability to climb and don't need any additional accessories to do so. They will happily climb their cage though they also enjoy toys that enable climbing.

Golden hamsters do require more attention than other types of hamsters since they tend to get easily stressed out by loud noises and bright lights.

These little creatures love playing around and exploring new things. If you want an active hamster who loves to play, then this might be your best bet.

DWARF HAMSTERS

Although all hamsters are cute and furry, there are reasons why many people prefer having a dwarf hamster over a regular one.

Besides being just plain cute, there are some practical benefits to choosing a dwarf hamster.

Dwarf hamsters will stay smaller throughout their lives. Their

smaller size means they will take up less space and have smaller appetites, so they're slightly easier and cheaper to care for than their Syrian cousins.

Dwarf hamsters come in a variety of different colours They are very small with short legs that make them look even cuter.

These hamsters can reach up to 3 inches long but most are between 2-3 inches.

They tend to have a shorter lifespan of 1.5 - 2 years so these animals may not live as long as their larger counterparts.

The most common types of dwarf hamsters are Campbell's Dwarf Hamsters, Winter White Hamsters, and Roborovski Hamsters. The Chinese hamster is also often categorised as a dwarf hamster due to being a similar size.

WINTER WHITE HAMSTERS

Winter white hamsters are also known as Siberian hamsters.

This type of hamster has been bred in captivity since the early 1900s.

Their coats grow long and can change colour to have an almost pure white colouration in the winter which gives them their name. This change rarely happens in captivity due to artificial lighting and heating which stops them from noticing the approaching winter.

The coat is usually a light grey with black stripes on the back and sides. These animals tend to be more active, playful and curious compared to other types of hamsters.

CAMPBELL'S DWARF

The Campbell's Dwarf is one of the most popular varieties and can grow up to 5 inches (12.5 cm) long while other dwarf hamsters only reach about 3-4 inches (10 cm).

This variety has been bred over many generations by selecting individuals with short legs and small bodies. These characteristics allow this type of hamster to be more agile than others so it can easily climb through its cage bars and escape.

They also have a very friendly personality which makes them ideal as indoor pets.

ROBOROVSKI HAMSTERS

Roborovski hamsters are active, agile creatures that make excellent pets for younger children. They are also commonly called Robo hamsters.

They can't be held as easily as other hamsters because they are so small (around 5cm or about the size of a little finger), but they make up for this with their friendliness towards people.

The fur on these hamsters is soft and silky making them look even cuter!

These hamsters very rarely bite and are not aggressive, preferring to run away rather than fight. They are difficult to tame or cuddle due to their speed and small size.

CHINESE HAMSTERS

Chinese hamsters are not true dwarf hamsters but are a similar size.

These small creatures come from China and Mongolia. They are small, furry, and have long tails.

They are very popular pets because of their friendly nature and ability to adapt well to any type of home environment.

They have a few disadvantages, such as they can be difficult to tame, and they can be aggressive. They are also less readily available in pet shops.

EQUIPMENT & SUPPLIES

Pet stores can be overwhelming. There are so many varieties of animals, toys, and accessories to choose from. As a first-time hamster owner, you may not know what equipment is necessary to buy for your pet. Here's some basic information on the things that will make life easier when it comes to caring for them.

The first thing you should buy is a cage. You will also need to buy bedding, a water bottle and food dishes. Your hamster will need an exercise wheel to keep active. It is possible to toilet train a hamster and litter boxes can be purchased for this purpose if desired.

A good idea for keeping your hamster exercised, happy, secure, and safe when out of its cage is an exercise ball. These balls are like little protective bubbles that allow them to explore their surroundings while keeping them both safe and easy to catch.

It's also a good idea to have a backup cage you can place them in while you clean their main cage or to transport the hamster to the vet for instance.

The best place to buy a hamster is at a local pet store. Hamsters at pet stores have been evaluated by experts and have been humanely treated before they were put up for sale. Pet shops are also able to provide advice about caring for your new friend.

If you're buying a baby hamster, make sure you know its age so you can be prepared with appropriately sized food and water dispensers when you bring home your little one.

CAGES

Hamsters need a lot of space to roam around in. A big cage will help your pet stay happy and healthy while it's awake.

The best way to keep your pet happy is to provide an interesting environment with lots of things to explore. Just like humans who need exercise in order to maintain good mental health, hamsters like having enrichment activities in their habitat such as tunnels and hiding places where they can explore during the day.

Cage size depends on how many hamsters you have but you should make sure there is at least two square feet per animal - around 1ft x 2 ft in total floor area or around 30cm x 60cm.

If possible, choose a cage with two levels; this will give them more room to move around.

If you choose a glass or plastic aquarium you must ensure it has plenty of ventilation to both allow enough air to circulate and to avoid the possibility of ammonia fumes building up and harming your hamster.

You may want to add extra hiding places inside the cage but it's also important not to overcrowd the cage with toys or bedding.

Smaller dwarf hamsters will be able to escape between the bars of a standard metal cage so a glass or plastic aquarium is more suitable for these varieties.

It should contain bedding material (such as shredded paper) and nesting materials such as cardboard tubes, plastic tubs, or even small boxes.

In the wild hamsters live in burrows so it's important to emulate this in their cages so your hamster feels secure.

PREPARING YOUR CAGE

1. To properly prepare a hamster cage it is a good idea to first line the bottom with old newspaper. This will absorb any spillages and messes and make it easier to clean the cage next time.

2. Next, you should add a bedding material such as wood chips or paper pellets. This layer should cover the floor of the cage and be around 3 inches deep so that your hamster can exercise their natural desire to burrow if they want.

3. You should provide somewhere private for your hamster to sleep so that they feel safe and secure, such as a small house or segregated area of the cage. This sleeping area can be lined with some soft cotton wool-like nesting material in order for your hamster to arrange as they like to make them feel snug.

4. You should provide a hamster wheel so that your hamster can burn off some energy and get enough exercise. Puzzle toys such as cardboard tubes, seesaws, or ladders will keep them amused.

5. Add a food bowl and fresh food. A ceramic bowl with shallow sides works best to ensure your hamster can reach the food and not tip it over easily.

6. Water dispensers ensure that the water remains clean and free of food and droppings. You should buy a chew and drip-proof dispenser which can be fixed to the side of the cage. Some dispensers can drip so it's a good idea to place them away from the main food, litter, and sleeping areas.

CLEANING YOUR CAGE

A hamsters cage should be cleaned thoroughly once a week.

Hamsters are really sensitive to smells, so you'll want to avoid strong-smelling things like citrus scents that might bother them.

All cleaning should be done with a mild scent-free soap or a hamster or pet-friendly cleaner which you can get from your local pet store.

1. Remove and replace all bedding and nesting material. Mix a clean dry piece of the old nesting material in with the new to help the hamster settle back into their clean cage.

2. Wash all of the food bowls and refill them with fresh food. Ensure all old food is removed.

3. If your hamster has been eating dry treats, it's best to change those for fresh ones too.

4. Finally, make sure there isn't anything in their cage that could hurt your hamster and give them plenty of space to move around.

CAGE PLACEMENT

You should place your cage on a stable surface. This should be away from:

- Your families sleeping areas
- Loud noises or anything that may startle your hamster
- Heaters
- Windows
- Direct sunlight
- Cold drafts
- Out of reach of other pets such as cats or dogs

The temperature around your hamster should remain consistent and ideally above 18 degrees Celsius (64 degrees Fahrenheit).

MASTERS OF ESCAPE!

A lot of people have heard the phrase "never let your hamster out of its cage." This is because hamsters are known for being escape artists.

They are crafty, persistent little creatures that will stop at nothing to get out of their cage. Once they're free, it's hard to catch them without sending them into a frenzy.

Hamsters can pop out of small spaces like between the bars of a cage and are always looking for ways to climb the walls.

A loose hamster can be very destructive. They can chew through wires and leave an unsightly mess of droppings. So it's important to keep a very close eye on them or ensure they're securely stored while you clean their cage.

A DAY IN THE LIFE OF YOUR HAMSTER

A day in the life of a hamster consists of many different tasks. It may not seem like it but hamsters have interesting lives and quite a busy schedule. They are naturally very clean animals and will groom themselves every day. The following is a list of daily routines that are common among most hamsters:

- Eating - Hamsters eat every 2-3 hours throughout the day.
- Sleeping - Most hamsters need around 12-14 hours of sleep each day. A good rule of thumb is if your hamster isn't sleeping during the day, he probably needs his rest too. Make sure they have plenty of hiding places where they can retreat from the sun or rain.
- Exercising - Hamsters love running on hamster wheels or playing with toys like tunnels and tubes. You should provide these as part of their routine so they don't get bored. Also, make sure that there are lots of different things for them to climb on and explore with.
- Playing with Toys - Hamsters enjoy playing with balls, ropes, cardboard boxes, plastic bottles, etc. Some people even use a small aquarium as an exercise toy. If you want to give him something more substantial than just playthings, consider getting some wood blocks or other types of puzzles. They will also be able to chew through those!
- Water - Your hamster needs water daily. There should always be fresh water available for drinking.

HAMSTERS AS PETS

Many people adopt hamsters as pets without realising that they are such intelligent and entertaining pets. Hamsters are often thought of as just a good starter pet for children, but they can actually bring hours of entertainment to their owners!

Having a pet in your home can bring hours of fun and entertainment. The best thing about a hamster is that they are

easy to care for and entertaining to watch! They are happy to explore their environment, enjoy petting from time to time, and can even learn tricks!

Hamsters make good pets because they are relatively low maintenance and don't require a lot of space. They are easy to care for because they don't need a great deal of space, live on a diet that is low in cost, and are very gentle by nature. These three traits make them a good pet for not only children but also people who have limited time to spend caring for an animal. Hamsters are generally friendly animals and will be happy if you give them attention. If you want your hamster to stay healthy, it's important to provide him with proper nutrition and exercise. This way he'll grow into a well-adjusted adult.

If you're looking for the perfect pet, a hamster could be a great choice. They are social, easy to care for, can be trained to do tricks, and most importantly, they are adorable. Hamsters come in many colours and sizes so no matter what your taste is, there's a hamster out there for you.

In conclusion, hamsters make great pets for anyone, and it is easy to care for them so long as you follow the guidelines set by your veterinarian. Make sure you know what type of hamster you are getting because it will vary in size, temperament, and other characteristics. Additionally, find out how many hamsters your home can accommodate before purchasing one or more!

Printed in Great Britain
by Amazon